This is the second, revised edition of a book first published in 1962, presenting 53 carols, a mixture of the old favourites with others deserving to be better known. The most familiar carols appear in their familiar settings, so that the book is of the maximum use to those who, year after year, have to organize or join carol parties with little or no rehearsal. At the same time the collection ventures judiciously into the European carol repertoire; prints the original words of all foreign carols in addition to the translations; and includes all the standard Christmas hymns. It is doubtful if so practical, yet wide ranging a collection can be found anywhere else at this modest price.

Mervyn Horder is a lifelong carol addict, music editor of a children's carol book, *On Christmas Day* (Longman, 1970), *A Book of Love Songs* (Duckworth, 1969), and composer of song cycles to words by John Betjeman (*Six Betjeman Songs*, 1966) and Dorothy Parker.

Cover design by Edward Ardizzoni

THE ORANGE
CAROL BOOK

ARRANGED BY MERVYN HORDER

SCHOTT & CO. LTD. LONDON

48 Great Marlborough Street London W1V 2BN

B. Schott's Söhne, Mainz—Editions Max Eschig, Paris

Schott Music Corporation, New York

First published 1962

Second edition 1973

Selection © 1962, 1973 by
MERVYN HORDER

Music of nos. 5 and 49 © 1962 by
MERVYN HORDER

Music of no. 53 © 1962 by
JOHN GARDNER

Musical setting of nos. 3, 4, 7, 8, 9, 11, 12, 13, 18,
20, 21, 22, 26, 27, 30, 35, 37, 38, 39, 41, 43, 44, 46,
48, 50, and 51 © 1962 by
MERVYN HORDER

ISBN 0 901938 10 6

Edition Schott 11235

Preface

No special claims are made for this collection of 53 Christmas carols, first published in 1962 and now presented in a second, revised edition. It represents not the deliberations of a committee of reverend scholars and musicologists but the labour of love of a single individual, albeit one with some years' experience of performing and listening to carols in all circumstances from the campfire to the concert hall. It is my wish to present those carols which it is most covenient for today's singers to find assembled between two covers. I do not believe that so practical a collection is assembled anywhere else, certainly not at so modest a price.

I do not apologize for including the standard Christmas hymns, or for having allowed myself to be guided largely by what is already established by usage in our hearts and affections. It is for this reason that, after ten years' experience with the first edition of this book, I have now replaced some of my own settings of well-known carols with the long established harmonizations by Stainer and Charles Wood. I aim for the collection to be particularly useful to the many of us who have to organize or join carol parties year after year at short notice, often with no rehearsal at all.

In far more instances than usual I have printed the original words of foreign carols alongside the English translation. In the singing of extra long carols, verses marked with an asterisk * may be omitted.

Acknowledgments. My thanks are due to the many copyright holders who have given permission for words or music or both to be included: these are acknowledged in detail in the footnote to each carol. I thank also Iris Holland Rogers and Sydney Carter who contributed new translations, and John Gardner who composed No. 53 specially for the book. All music settings not otherwise acknowledged are by me. As before, and at all times, my thanks are due to Dorothy Playsted, George Dyson, Hubert Middleton, H. Waldo Warner and Arthur Pritchard who have taught me music.

If the singing of these carols gives you one half the pleasure that the assembling of them has given me, I shall be happy.

London   M. H.
Christmas 1972

THE ORANGE CAROL BOOK

1. All Poor Men and Humble

All poor men and hum-ble, All lame men who stum-ble, Come
For Je-sus, our treas-ure, with love past all meas-ure, In

haste ye, nor feel ye a - fraid; Though wise men who found him Laid
low-ly poor man-ger was laid. Then haste we to show him The

rich gifts a - round him, Yet ox - en they gave him their
prais - es we owe him; Our ser - vice he ne'er can de -

hay: And Je - sus in beau-ty Ac - cep-ted their
spise: Whose love still is a - ble To show us that

du - ty; Con - ten - ted in man - ger he lay.
sta - ble Where soft - ly in man - ger he lies.

Welsh traditional words 'O Deued Pob Cristion', translated by K. E. Roberts, reprinted from the *Oxford Book of Carols* by permission of the Oxford University Press. The traditional tune to these words, 'Olwen', set by Dr Caradog Roberts, is printed by permission of the Caniedydd Committee, Welsh Congregational Union.

2. Angels from the Realms of Glory

Come and wor - ship
Glo - ri - a

Christ the new - born King. Come
in ex - cel - sis De - o, Glo - ri - a

and wor - ship, Wor - ship Christ, the new - born King.
ri - a in ex - cel - sis De - o.

ANGELS, from the realms of glory
Wing your flight o'er all the earth;
Ye who sang creation's story
Now proclaim Messiah's birth:
  Come and worship Christ the new-born King.
  Come and worship, Worship Christ, the new-born King.

2. Shepherds, in the field abiding,
    Watching o'er your flocks by night,
  God with man is now residing,
    Yonder shines the Infant Light:

*3. Sages, leave your contemplations,
    Brighter visions beam afar;
  Seek the great Desire of nations;
    Ye have seen His natal star:

*4. Saints, before the altar bending,
    Watching long in hope and fear,
  Suddenly the Lord descending
    In His temple shall appear:

5. Though an infant now we view Him,
    He shall fill His Father's throne,
  Gather all the nations to Him;
    Every knee shall then bow down:

LES anges dans nos campagnes
Ont entonné l'hymne des cieux,
Et l'écho de nos montagnes
Redit ce chant mélodieux:
  Gloria in excelsis Deo,
  Gloria in excelsis Deo.

2. Bergers, pour qui cette fête?
  Quel est l'objet de tous ces chants?
  Quel vainqueur, quelle conquête
  Mérite ces cris triomphants?

3. Ils annoncent la naissance
  Du libérateur d'Israel,
  Et, pleins de reconnaissance,
  Chantent en ce jour solennel:

*4. Bergers, loin de vos retraites
  Unissez-vous à leurs concerts,
  Et que vos tendres musettes
  Fassent retentir dans les airs:

*5. Cherchons tous l'heureux village
  Qui l'a vu naître sous ses toits;
  Offrons-lui le tendre hommage
  Et de nos coeurs et de nos voix!

The English words by J. Montgomery, 1825, appear to be loosely modelled on the original French 18th century version to which the tune belongs. Setting by Martin Shaw reprinted from the *Oxford Book of Carols* by permission of the Oxford University Press. The more singable refrain of the French version may be used in place of the English refrain.

3. A Virgin Most Pure

Aye and there fore be mer - ry, Set sor - rows a - side; Christ Je - - sus our Sa - viour was born on this tide.

A Virgin most pure, as the prophets do tell,
Hath brought forth a baby, as it hath befel,
To be our Redeemer from death, hell and sin,
Which Adam's trangression hath wrappèd us in.

Aye and therefore be merry,
Set sorrows aside:
Christ Jesus our Saviour was born on this tide.

2. At Bethlem in Jewry a city there was,
   Where Joseph and Mary together did pass,
   And there to be taxèd with many one mo',
   For Caesar commanded the same should be so:

*3. But when they had entered the city so fair,
   A number of people so mighty was there,
   That Joseph and Mary, whose substance was small,
   Could find in the inn there no lodging at all:

4. Then were they constrained in a stable to lie,
   Where horses and asses they used for to tie;
   Their lodging so simple they took it no scorn:
   But against the next morning our Saviour was born:

*5. The King of all kings to this world being brought,
   Small store of fine linen to wrap him was sought;
   And when she had swaddled her young son so sweet,
   Within an ox-manger she laid him to sleep:

*6. Then God sent an angel from Heaven so high,
   To certain poor shepherds in fields where they lie,
   And bade them no longer in sorrow to stay,
   Because that our Saviour was born on this day:

7. Then presently after the shepherds did spy
   A number of angels that stood in the sky;
   They joyfully talkèd, and sweetly did sing,
   To God be all glory, our heavenly King:

This carol appears complete in D. Gilbert, *Some Ancient
Christmas Carols*, 1822; but the tune used here is the
telescoped version first popularised by Bramley and
Stainer, *Christmas Carols*, 1871

4. Away in a Manger 38

AWAY in a manger, no crib for a bed,
The little Lord Jesus laid down his sweet head;
The stars in the bright sky looked down where he lay,
The little Lord Jesus asleep on the hay.

The cattle are lowing, the baby awakes;
But little Lord Jesus, no crying he makes;
I love thee, Lord Jesus! Look down from the sky,
And stay by my bedside till morning is nigh.

Be near me, Lord Jesus; I ask thee to stay
Close by me for ever, and love me, I pray:
Bless all the dear children in thy tender care,
And fit us for Heaven to live with thee there.

Words anonymous American, first known 1885. Tune by
W. J. Kirkpatrick, 1895. Both tune and words have at
various times been wrongly ascribed to Martin Luther.

5. Brightest and Best

B<small>RIGHTEST</small> and best of the sons of the morning,
Dawn on our darkness, and lend us thine aid,
Star of the east, the horizon adorning,
Guide where our infant Redeemer is laid!

2. Cold on His cradle the dewdrops are shining,
Low lies His head with the beasts of the stall;
Angels adore Him, in slumber reclining,
Maker, and Monarch, and Saviour of all.

3. Say, shall we yield Him, in costly devotion,
Odours of Edom and offerings divine;
Gems of the mountain, and pearls of the ocean,
Myrrh from the forest, or gold from the mine?

4. Vainly we offer each ample oblation,
Vainly with gifts would His favour secure;
Richer by far is the heart's adoration,
Dearer to God are the prayers of the poor.

5. Brightest and best of the sons of the morning,
Dawn on our darkness, and lend us thine aid,
Star of the east, the horizon adorning,
Guide where our infant Redeemer is laid!

Words, 1811, by Reginald Heber. Tune 'Edom' by M. H., 1956.

6. Behold a Rose is Springing

BEHOLD a rose is springing
Upon this holy tree,
Our elders thus were singing
Of Jesse's line to be:
A rosebud pure and white
Deep in the cold midwinter
Upon the dark midnight.

2. This rose foretold in story
Springs as Isaiah said,
Bringing to us the glory
Of Mary perfect maid;
Through God's own power and might
Hath she brought forth her flower
Upon the dark midnight.

3. O hear us, gracious mother,
Sweet Mary, tender rose,
Through all thy Son did suffer,
His sorrows and his woes,
Help us prepare a bower
Within our hearts to cherish
This pure and perfect flower.

Es ist ein' Ros' entsprungen
Aus einer Wurzel zart,
Als uns die Alten sungen:
Aus Jesse kam die Art;
Und hat ein Blümlein bracht,
Mitten im kalten Winter,
Wohl zu der halben Nacht.

2. Das Röslein, das ich meine,
Davon Jesaias sagt,
Ist Maria die reine,
Die uns dies Blümlein bracht;
Aus Gottes ew'gem Rat
Hat sie ein Kindlein g'boren
Ist blieb'n ein' reine Magd.

3. Wir bitten dich von Herzen,
Maria, Rose zart,
Durch dieses Blümleins Schmerzen,
Die er empfunden hat,
Wollst uns behülflich sein,
Dass wir ihm mögen machen
Ein' Wohnung hübsch und fein!

FLOS de radice Jesse
Est natus hodie,
Quem nobis jam adesse
Laetamur unice.
Flos ille Jesus est,
Maria virgo radix
De qua flos ortus est.

2. Hunc Isaïas florem
Praesagus cecinit,
Ad eius nos amorem
Nascentis allicit.
Flos fructum superat;
Coeli terraeque cives
Flos ille recreat.

3. Hic suo flos odore
Fideles attrahit,
Divino mox amore
Attractos imbuit.
O flos, o gratia!
Ad te, ad te suspiro,
Me de te satia.

15th century Latin words and tune, harmonised by
Michael Pretorius, 1609. English words translated from
the German by Iris Holland Rogers, 1961.

7. Blow the Trumpet and Bang the Drum

Blow the trum-pet and bang the drum, Set all the bells in the steep-le ring-ing,

Blow the trum-pet and bang the drum: Tell the world that the Boy has come.

End

to 𝄋

Blow the trumpet and bang the drum,
Set all the bells in the steeple ringing,
Blow the trumpet and bang the drum:
Tell the world that the Boy has come.

* THROUGH four thousand years of night
    There were priests and prophets singing,
Through four thousand years of night
'He will come with the morning light.'

2. O how charming, O how gay,
    All our hearts with his sweetness winning,
    O how charming, O how gay
    Christ the Boy in his cradle lay!

3. In a manger rolled in hay,
    To mankind its ransom bringing,
    In a manger rolled in hay
    God his Godhead puts away.

4. Boy and King we kneel before,
    While the bells in the sky are ringing,
    Boy and King we kneel before,
    Be our ruler for evermore!

> *Il est né le divin Enfant,*
> *Jouez hautbois, résonnez musettes;*
> *Il est né le divin Enfant,*
> *Chantons tous son avènement.*

DEPUIS plus de quatre mille ans
    Nous le promettaient les prophètes,
Depuis plus de quatre mille ans
Nous attendions cet heureux temps.

2. Ah! qu'il est beau, qu'il est charmant,
    Ah! que ses grâces sont parfaites!
    Ah! qu'il est beau, qu'il est charmant,
    Qu'il est doux ce divin Enfant!

3. Une étable est son logement,
    Un peu de paille est sa couchette,
    Une étable est son logement,
    Pour un Dieu quel abaissement.

4. O Jésus, ô Roi tout puissant,
    Si petit enfant que vous êtes,
    O Jésus, ô Roi tout puissant,
    Régnez sur nous entièrement.

* Traditional French 18th century words and tune.
  English paraphrase by Sydney Carter, 1961.*

For singing by very young children, the first verse
may be omitted.

8. Cherry Tree Carol

AS Joseph was a-walking
He heard an Angel sing:
'This night there shall be born
Our gracious Heav'nly King;

2. 'He neither shall be born
In housen nor in hall,
Nor in the place of Paradise,
But in an ox's stall.

3. 'He neither shall be clothèd
In purple nor in pall;
But all in fair white linen
As wear sweet babies all.

4. 'He neither shall be rockèd
In silver nor in gold;
But in a wooden cradle
That rocks upon the mould.

5. 'He neither shall be christen'd
In white wine nor in red;
But with the fair spring water,
With which we were christenèd.'

6. As Joseph was a-walking,
Thus did the Angel sing;
And Mary's Child at midnight
Was born to be our King.

Words and tune traditional English.

9. Coventry Carol

L ULLAY, lullay, thou little tiny child,
By by, lully, lullay,
Lully, lullay, thou tiny child,
By by, lully, lullay.

2. O sisters too, how may we do,
   For to preserve this day
   This poor youngling for whom we sing
   By by, lully, lullay?

3. Herod the king in his raging,
   Chargèd he hath this day
   His men of might, in his own sight,
   All children young to slay.

4. Then woe is me, poor child, for thee,
   And ever morn and day
   For Thy parting nor say nor sing
   By by, lully, lullay.

Words (1534) and tune (1591) from the pageant of the
Shearmen and Tailors' Company at Coventry, both
modernised. The F/F sharp clash in the last line appears
in the 1591 version of the tune, but may be a copyist's
error.

10. Christians, Awake

CHRISTIANS, awake, salute the happy morn
Whereon the Saviour of mankind was born;
Rise to adore the mystery of love,
Which hosts of angels chanted from above;
With them the joyful tidings first begun
Of God incarnate and the virgin's son.

2. Then to the watchful shepherds it was told,
Who heard the angelic herald's voice, 'Behold
I bring you tidings of a Saviour's birth
To you and all the nations upon earth:
This day hath God fulfilled His promised word,
This day is born a Saviour, Christ the Lord.'

*3. He spake; and straightway the celestial choir
In hymns of joy, unknown before, conspire:
The praises of redeeming love they sang,
And heaven's whole orb with alleluias rang:
God's highest glory was their anthem still,
Peace upon earth, and unto men goodwill.

*4. To Bethlehem straight the enlightened shepherds ran,
To see the wonder God had wrought for man,
And found, with Joseph and the Blessèd Maid,
Her Son, the Saviour, in a manger laid:
Then to their flocks, still praising God, return,
And their glad hearts with holy rapture burn.

5. O may we keep and ponder in our mind
God's wondrous love in saving lost mankind;
Trace we the Babe, who hath retrieved our loss,
From His poor manger to His bitter cross;
Tread in his steps, assisted by his grace,
Till man's first heavenly state again takes place.

6. Then may we hope, the angelic thrones among,
To sing, redeemed, a glad triumphal song;
He that was born upon this joyful day,
Around us all His glory shall display;
Saved by His love, incessant shall we sing
Eternal praise to heaven's Almighty King.

Words by J. Byrom, 1749, said to have been a Christmas
present for his daughter. Tune 'Stockport' by John
Wainwright, 1750.

11. Christ was Born on Christmas Day

1. Christ was born on Christ-mas Day; Wreathe the hol - ly, twine the bay.
2. He is born to set us free, He is born our Lord to be.
3. Let the bright red ber - ries glow. Ev - ery where in good - ly show;
4. Chris - tian men, re - joice and sing; 'Tis the birth - day of a King,

Chris-tus na-tus ho - di - e: The Babe, the Son, the Ho - ly One of Ma - ry.
Ex Ma - ri - a vir-gin - e: The God, the Lord, by all a-dored for e - ver.
Chris-tus na - tus ho - di - e: The Babe, the Son, the Ho - ly One of Ma - ry.
Ex Ma - ri - a vir-gin - e: The God, the Lord, by all a-dored for e - ver.

5. Night of sad - ness, morn of glad - ness e - ver-more: E - ver, e - ver:

Af - ter ma - ny trou -bles sore, Morn of glad-ness e - ver-more and e - ver-more.

16

6. Mid-night scarce-ly past and o-ver, Draw-ing to this ho-ly morn:

Ve-ry ear-ly, ve-ry ear-ly Christ was born. 7. Sing out with bliss, His

Name is this: Em-man-u-el: As was fore-told in

days of old by Ga-bri-el. 8. Mid-night scarce-ly past and o-ver,

Draw-ing to this ho-ly morn: Ve-ry ear-ly, ve-ry ear-ly Christ was born.

Words by J. M. Neale for the old German tune 'Resonet in Laudibus'.

12. Come All You Worthy Gentlemen

COME all you worthy gentlemen,
That may be standing by,
Christ our blessed Saviour
Was born on Christmas Day.
The blessed Virgin Mary.
Unto the Lord did pray.
O we wish you the comfort and tidings of joy!

2. Christ our blessed Saviour
Now in the manger lay –
He's lying in the manger,
While oxen feed on hay.
The blessed Virgin Mary
Unto the Lord did pray.
O we wish you the comfort and tidings of joy!

3. God bless the ruler of this house,
And long on may he reign,
Many happy Christmases
He live to see again!
God bless our generation,
Who live both far and near,
And we wish them a happy, a happy New Year.

Words and tune collected by Cecil Sharp in Bridgwater,
Somerset, 1913, and reprinted by permission of Novello
& Co Ltd.

13. Deck the Halls

(♩ = 116)

1. Deck the halls with boughs of hol-ly,
2. See the blaz-ing Yule be-fore us,   *Fa la, la, la, la, fa   la, la, la,*
3. Fast a-way the old year pas-ses,

'Tis the sea-son to be jol-ly,
Strike the harp and join the cho-rus,   *Fa la, la, la, la,   fa   la, la, la,*
Hail the new, ye lads and las-ses,

Don we now our gay ap-pa-rel,
Fol-low me in mer-ry meas-ure,   *Fa   la,   la,   la,   la, la, la,*
Sing we joy-ous all to-geth-er,

Troll the an-cient Yule-tide ca-rol,
While I tell of Yule-tide treas-ure,   *Fa   la, la, la, la, fa   la, la, la.*
Heed-less of the wind and weath-er,

Words and tune 'Hobaderrydanno' are both Welsh traditional.

20

14. Ding Dong Merrily on High

DING dong! merrily on high   in heav'n the bells are ringing:
Ding dong! verily the sky   is riv'n with Angel singing.
Gloria, Hosanna in excelsis!

2. E'en so here below, below   let steeple bells be swungen,
And i-o, i-o, i-o   by priest and people sungen.
Gloria, Hosanna in excelsis!

3. Pray you, dutifully prime   your Matin chime, ye ringers;
May you beautifully rime   your Evetime song, ye singers:
Gloria, Hosanna in excelsis!

Tune 'Branle de l'Official' from Thoinot Arbeau's
Orchésographie, 1588. Words by G. R. Woodward and
setting by Charles Wood from *The Cambridge Carol
Book,* 1924, by permission of the S.P.C.K.

15. God Rest You Merry, Gentlemen

GOD rest you merry, gentlemen,
Let nothing you dismay,
Remember Christ our Saviour
Was born on Christmas Day,
To save us all from Satan's power
When we were gone astray;
  O tidings of comfort and joy, comfort and joy,
  O tidings of comfort and joy.

*2. In Bethlehem, in Jewry,
This blessèd Babe was born,
And laid within a manger,
Upon this blessèd morn;
The which His Mother Mary
Did nothing take in scorn.

3. From God our Heavenly Father
A blessèd angel came;
And unto certain shepherds
Brought tidings of the same:
How that in Bethlehem was born
The Son of God by Name.

*4. "Fear not," then said the angel,
"Let nothing you affright,
This day is born a Saviour
Of a pure Virgin bright,
So frequently to vanquish all
The fiends of Satan quite."

5. The shepherds at those tidings
Rejoicèd much in mind,
And left their flocks a-feeding,
In tempest, storm, and wind:
And went to Bethlehem straightway,
The Son of God to find.

*6. And when they came to Bethlehem
Where our dear Saviour lay,
They found Him in a manger,
Where oxen feed on hay;
His Mother Mary kneeling down,
Unto the Lord did pray.

7. Now to the Lord sing praises,
All you within this place,
And with true love and brotherhood
Each other now embrace;
The holy tide of Christmas
All other doth deface.

Words and tune traditional, the latter first printed 1846.
Harmony by Sir John Stainer, with added final bars.

16. Good King Wenceslas

GOOD King Wenceslas looked out
  On the Feast of Stephen,
When the snow lay round about,
Deep, and crisp, and even;
Brightly shone the moon that night,
Though the frost was cruel,
When a poor man came in sight,
Gathering winter fuel.

2. "Hither, page, and stand by me,
  If thou know'st it, telling,
Yonder peasant, who is he?
Where and what his dwelling?"
"Sire, he lives a good league hence,
Underneath the mountain;
Right against the forest fence,
By St. Agnes' fountain."

3. "Bring me flesh, and bring me wine,
  Bring me pine-logs hither;
Thou and I will see him dine,
When we bear them thither."

Page and monarch forth they went,
Forth they went together;
Through the rude wind's wild lament,
And the bitter weather.

4. "Sire, the night is darker now,
  And the wind blows stronger;
Fails my heart, I know not how,
I can go no longer."
"Mark my footsteps, good my page!
Tread thou in them boldly:
Thou shalt find the winter's rage
Freeze thy blood less coldly."

5. In his master's steps he trod,
  Where the snow lay dinted;
Heat was in the very sod
Which the saint had printed.
Therefore, Christian men, be sure,
Wealth or rank possessing,
Ye who now will bless the poor,
Shall yourselves find blessing.

Words by J. M. Neale, 1853, to fit the tune of a Spring carol 'Tempus Adest Floridum' appearing in the collection *Piae Cantiones*, 1582. The legend is from Bohemia. Harmony by Sir John Stainer.

17. Green Grow'th the Holly

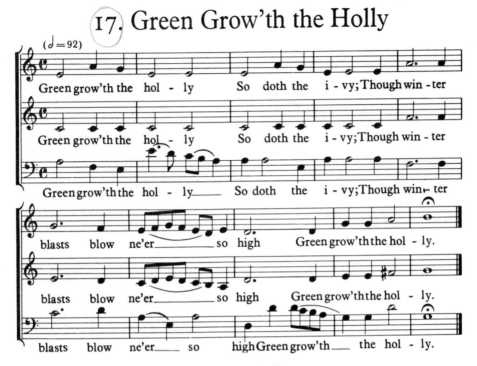

(♩=92)

Green grow'th the hol - ly   So doth the   i - vy; Though win - ter
blasts   blow   ne'er_____ so high   Green grow'th the hol - ly.

G REEN grow'th the holly
So doth the ivy;
Though winter blasts blow ne'er so high
Green grow'th the holly.

2. Gay are the flowers,
Hedgerows and ploughlands;
The days grow longer in the sun,
Soft fall the showers.

3. Full gold thy harvest,
Grain for thy labour;
With God must work for daily bread,
Else, man, thou starvest.

4. Fast fall the shed leaves,
Russet and yellow;
But resting-buds are snug and safe
Where swung the dead leaves.

5. Green grow'th the holly,
So doth the ivy;
The God of life can never die,
Hope! saith the holly.

The tune, a 16th century love-song attributed to Henry VIII, has been transcribed by Lady Mary Trefusis, with words added; reprinted from the *Oxford Book of Carols* by permission of the Oxford University Press.

25

18. Greensleeves

To be sung in unison

26

THE Old Year now away is fled,
    The New Year it is enterèd;
Then let us all our sins down-tread
And joyfully all appear:
Let's merry be this day,
And let us now with sport and play
Hang grief, cast care away!
God send you a happy New Year!

2. The name-day now of Christ we keep,
    Who for our sins did often weep;
His hands and feet were wounded deep
And his blessèd side with a spear;
His head they crowned with thorn,
And at him they did laugh and scorn,
Who for our good was born:
God send you a happy New Year!

3. And now with New Year's gifts each friend
    Unto each other they do send;
God grant we may all our lives amend,
And that the truth may appear.
Now, like the snake, your skin
Cast off, of evil thoughts and sin,
And so the year begin:
God send you a happy New Year!

WHAT Child is this, who, laid to rest,
    On Mary's lap is sleeping?
Whom angels greet with anthems sweet,
While shepherds watch are keeping?
This, this is Christ the King;
Whom shepherds guard and angels sing:
Haste, haste to bring Him laud,
The Babe, the Son of Mary!

2. Why lies He in such mean estate,
    Where ox and ass are feeding?
Good Christian, fear: for sinners here
The silent Word is pleading:
Nails, spear, shall pierce Him through,
The Cross be borne, for me, for you:
Hail, hail, the Word made flesh,
The Babe, the Son of Mary!

3. So bring Him incense, gold, and myrrh,
    Come peasant, King to own Him;
The King of kings salvation brings;
Let loving hearts enthrone Him.
Raise, raise, the song on high,
The Virgin sings her lullaby:
Joy, joy, for Christ is born,
The Babe, the Son of Mary!

Tune traditional. The first set of words is from *New
Christmas Carols*, 1642, in the collection of Anthony à
Wood; the second is by W. Chatterton Dix, 1861.

19. Hark! the Herald Angels Sing

HARK! the herald angels sing
   Glory to the new-born King;
Peace on earth, and mercy mild,
God and sinners reconciled:
Joyful, all ye nations, rise:
Join the triumph of the skies,
With the angelic host proclaim,
Christ is born in Bethlehem:

Hark! the herald angels sing
Glory to the new-born King.

2. Christ by highest heaven adored,
   Christ the everlasting Lord,
   Late in time behold Him come,
   Offspring of a virgin's womb:
   Veiled in flesh the Godhead see;
   Hail the incarnate Deity,
   Pleased as man with men to dwell,
   Jesus, our Immanuel:

Hark! the herald angels sing
Glory to the new-born King.

3. Hail the heaven-born Prince of peace!
   Hail the Sun of righteousness!
   Light and life to all He brings,
   Risen with healing in His wings:
   Mild He lays His glory by,
   Born that man no more may die,
   Born to raise the sons of earth,
   Born to give them second birth:

Hark! the herald angels sing
Glory to the new-born King.

Words originally by Charles Wesley, 1739, beginning
'Hark how all the welkin rings, With glory to the King
of kings'; altered by various hands to its present form
about 1810. The tune 'St. Vincent' was adapted by
W. H. Cummings (1856) from a chorus in Mendelssohn's
Festgesang (1840); Mendelssohn didn't like it.

20. Here We Come a-Wassailing

Love and joy come to you And to you your was-sail too, And God bless you and send___ you A hap - py New Year, And God send___ you a hap-py New___ Year.

HERE we come a-wassailing
Among the leaves so green,
Here we come a-wandering,
So fair to be seen:

*Love and joy come to you
And to you your wassail too,
And God bless you, and send you
A happy New Year,
And God send you a happy New Year.*

*2. Our wassail cup is made
Of the rosemary tree,
And so is your beer
Of the best barley:

3. We are not daily beggars
That beg from door to door,
But we are neighbours' children
Whom you have seen before:

*4. Call up the butler of this house,
Put on his golden ring;
Let him bring us up a glass of beer,
And better shall we sing:

*5. We have got a little purse
Of ratching leather skin;
We want a little of your money
To line it well within:

6. Bring us out a table,
And spread it with a cloth;
Bring us out a mouldy cheese,
And some of your Christmas loaf:

7. God bless the master of this house,
Likewise the mistress too;
And all the little children
That round the table go:

Words from Husk, *Songs of the Nativity*, 1868.
Tune traditional from Yorkshire.

21. How Far is it to Bethlehem?

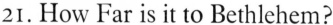

HOW far is it to Bethlehem? Not very far.
  Shall we find the stable-room Lit by a star?

2. Can we see the little child, Is he within?
   If we lift the wooden latch, May we go in?

3. May we stroke the creatures there, Ox, ass and sheep?
   May we peep like them and see Jesus asleep?

4. If we touch his tiny hand, Will he awake?
   Will he know we've come so far Just for his sake?

5. Great kings have precious gifts, And we have nought,
   Little smiles and little tears Are all we brought.

6. For all weary children Mary must weep.
   Here, on his bed of straw Sleep, children, sleep.

7. God in his mother's arms, Babes in the byre,
   Sleep, as they sleep who find Their heart's desire.

Words by Frances Chesterton, reprinted by permission
of the copyright-holder, Miss D. E. Collins. The tune
'Stowey' is traditional from Somerset.

22. I Saw Three Ships

I saw three ships come sailing in,
On Christmas Day, on Christmas Day,
I saw three ships come sailing in,
On Christmas Day in the morning.

2. And what was in those ships all three?

3. Our Saviour Christ and his lady.

4. Pray, whither sailed those ships all three?

5. O, they sailed into Bethlehem.

*6. And all the bells in earth shall ring,

*7. And all the angels in Heaven shall sing,

*8. And all the souls on earth shall sing,

9. Then let us all rejoice amain!

Words and tune English traditional.

23. In Dulci Jubilo

*I*N dulci jubilo
　Let us our homage shew;
Our heart's joy reclineth
　In praesepio,
And like a bright star shineth
　Matris in gremio.
Alpha es et O,
　Alpha es et O.

2. *O Jesu parvule!*
　My heart is sore for Thee!
Hear me I beseech Thee,
　O puer optime!
My prayer let it reach Thee,
　O princeps gloriae!
Trahe me post Te!
　Trahe me post Te!

3. *O patris caritas!*
　O nati lenitas!
Deep were we stainèd
　Per nostra crimina;
But Thou hast for us gainèd
　Coelorum gaudia.
O that we were there,
　O that we were there!

4. *Ubi sunt gaudia*
　If that they be not there?
Angels there are singing
　Nova cantica,
Sweet bells the while aringing
　In regis curia:
O that we were there,
　O that we were there!

*I*N dulci jubilo,
　Nun singet und seid fro!
Unsers herzen wunne
　Leit *in praesepio*
Und leuchtet als die Sonne
　Matris in gremio.
Alpha es et O!
　Alpha es et O!

2. *O Jesu parvule*
　Nach dir ist mir so Weh!
Tröst mir mein Gemüte
　O puer optime!
Durch alle deine Güte
　O princeps gloriae!
Trahe me post te!
　Trahe me post te!

3. *O patris caritas!*
　O nati lenitas!
Wir weren all verloren
　Per nostra crimina
So hat er uns erworben
　Coelorum gaudia.
Eia wer wir da!
　Eia wer wir da!

4. *Ubi sunt gaudia*
　Nirgend mehr denn da!
Da die Engel singen
　Nova cantica
Und die Schellen klingen
　In regis curia!
Eia wer wir da!
　Eia wer wir da!

Original German-Latin words and tune, 1570, and probably earlier. English translation and setting by R. L. Pearsall, 1837.

24. In the Bleak Midwinter

($\bullet$ = 72)

1. In the bleak mid - win - ter Frosty wind made moan,
2. Our God, heaven can - not hold Him Nor earth sus - tain;
3. An - gels and arch - an - gels May have gath - ered there,
4. What can I give Him, Poor as I am?

Earth stood hard as ir - on, Wa - ter like a - stone
Heaven and earth shall flee a - way When He comes to reign:
Cher - ub - im and ser - aph - im Throng - èd the air; But
If I were a shep - herd I would bring a lamb;

Snow had fal - len, snow on snow, Snow on snow,
In the bleak mid - win - ter A sta - ble place suf - ficed
on - ly His Moth - er, In her maid - en bliss,
If I were a wise man, I would do my part; Yet

In the bleak mid - win - ter, Long a - go.
The Lord God al - migh - ty, Jes - us Christ.
Wor-shipped the Be - lov - èd With a kiss.
what I can I give him Give my heart.

IN the bleak mid-winter
   Frosty wind made moan,
Earth stood hard as iron,
Water like a stone;
Snow had fallen, snow on snow,
Snow on snow,
In the bleak mid-winter,
Long ago.

2. Our God, heaven cannot hold Him,
   Nor earth sustain;
   Heaven and earth shall flee away
   When He comes to reign:
   In the bleak mid-winter
   A stable-place sufficed
   The Lord God almighty,
   Jesus Christ.

3. Angels and archangels
   May have gathered there,
   Cherubim and seraphim
   Throngèd the air;
   But only His mother,
   In her maiden bliss,
   Worshipped the Belovèd
   With a kiss.

4. What can I give Him,
   Poor as I am?
   If I were a shepherd,
   I would bring a lamb;
   If I were a wise man,
   I would do my part;
   Yet what I can I give Him—
   Give my heart.

Words by Christina Rossetti 'before 1872', with one verse omitted. Tune 'Cranham' by Gustav Holst, printed here by kind permission of Miss Imogen Holst and the composer's Trustees.

25. It Came upon the Midnight Clear

IT came upon the midnight clear,
That glorious song of old,
From angels bending near the earth
To touch their harps of gold:
'Peace on the earth, goodwill to men,
From heaven's all-gracious King';
The world in solemn stillness lay
To hear the angels sing.

2. Still through the cloven skies they come,
With peaceful wings unfurled,
And still their heavenly music floats
O'er all the weary world:
Above its sad and lowly plains
They bend on hovering wing,
And ever o'er its Babel sounds
The blessèd angels sing.

*3. Yet with the woes of sin and strife
The world has suffered long,
Beneath the angel-strain have rolled
Two thousand years of wrong;
And man, at war with man, hears not
The love-song which they bring:
O hush the noise, ye men of strife,
And hear the angels sing.

4. For lo! the days are hastening on,
By prophet bards foretold,
When with the ever-circling years
Comes round the age of gold;
When peace shall over all the earth
Its ancient splendours fling,
And the whole world send back the song
Which now the angels sing.

Words by E. H. Sears, a Unitarian minister from Mas-
sachusetts, 1849. Tune 'Noel' by Arthur Sullivan, 1874;
probably the second half only is Sullivan's original work.

26. Infant Holy (Polish Carol)

1. In-fant ho - ly, In-fant low - ly, For his bed a cat - tle stall; Ox - en low - ing, lit - tle know - ing Christ the Babe is Lord of all. Swift are wing - ing an - gels sing - ing, No-wells ring - ing, ti - dings bring -ing, Christ the Babe is Lord of all, Christ the Babe is Lord of all.

2. Flocks were sleep - ing, Shep herds keep - ing vi - gil till the mor - ning new, Saw the glo - ry, heard the sto - ry, Ti - dings of a gos - pel true. Thus re - joic - ing, free from sor - row, Praises voic - ing, greet the mor-row, Christ the Babe was born for you, Christ the Babe was born for you.

Words and tune traditional Polish. English translation by E. M. G. Reed, printed by permission of Evans Brothers Ltd.

27. Joy to the World

JOY to the World; the Lord is come; Let Earth receive her King:
Let every Heart prepare Him Room,
And Heaven and Nature sing, and Heaven and Nature sing,
And Heaven, and Heaven and Nature sing.

2. Joy to the Earth, the Saviour reigns; Let Men their Songs employ;
While Fields and Floods, Rocks, Hills and Plains
Repeat the sounding Joy, Repeat the sounding Joy,
Repeat, repeat the sounding Joy.

3. He rules the World with Truth and Grace, and makes the Nations prove
The Glories of His Righteousness,
And Wonders of His Love, and Wonders of His Love,
And Wonders, and Wonders of His Love.

Words by Isaac Watts, *The Psalms of David*, 1719; this
is a paraphrase of Psalm 98, with one verse omitted. The
tune, popular in U.S.A., is sometimes attributed there to
Handel.

28. King Jesus hath a Garden

There

naught is heard but pa - ra - dise bird, Harp, dul - ci - mer, lute, With

cym - bal,___ trump and tym - bal, And the ten-der, sooth-ing flute.With

cym - bal,___ trump and tym - bal, And the ten-der, sooth-ing flute.___

K ING Jesus hath a garden full of divers flowers,
Where I go culling posies gay all times and hours.

There naught is heard but paradise bird,
Harp, dulcimer, lute,
With cymbal, trump and tymbal,
And the tender, soothing flute.

2. The Lily, white in blossom there, is Chastity:
The Violet, with sweet perfume, Humility.

*3. The bonny Damask-rose is known as Patience;
The blithe and thrifty Marygold, Obedience.

*4. The Crown Imperial bloometh too in yonder place
'Tis Charity, of stock divine, the flower of grace.

5. Yet, 'mid the brave, the bravest prize of all may claim
The Star of Bethlem—JESUS—blessèd be His Name!

6. Ah! Jesu Lord, my heal and weal, my bliss complete,
Make Thou my heart Thy garden-plot, fair, trim and neat.

That I may hear This musick clear:
Harp, dulcimer, lute,
With cymbal, trump and tymbal,
And the tender, soothing flute.

Words translated by G. R. Woodward from the 17th
century Dutch carol *Heer Jesus heeft een Hofken,* with
the proper tune arranged by Charles Wood. Both are
reprinted from *The Cowley Carol Book* by permission
of A. R. Mowbray & Co. Ltd.

29. O Come, All Ye Faithful

O come, let us a - dore Him, O come, let us a -
Ve - ni - te a - dor - e - mus, Ve - ni - te a - dor -

dore Him, O come, let us a - dore Him,— Christ,— the Lord.
e - mus, Ve - ni - te a - dor - e - mus,— Do - min - um.

O come, all ye faithful,
  Joyful and triumphant,
O come ye, O come ye to Bethlehem;
Come and behold Him,
Born the King of Angels;

O come, let us adore Him,
O come, let us adore Him,
O come, let us adore Him,
Christ, the Lord.

2. God of God,
  Light of Light,
Lo, He abhors not the Virgin's womb.
Very God,
Begotten, not created:

  O come, &c.

3. Sing, choirs of Angels,
  Sing in exultation,
Sing, all ye citizens of heaven above,
Glory to God
In the highest:

  O come, &c.

4. Yea, Lord, we greet Thee,
  Born this happy morning.
Jesu, to Thee be glory given;
Word of the Father,
Now in flesh appearing:

  O come, &c.

ADESTE, fideles,
  Laeti triumphantes;
Venite, venite in Bethlehem:
Natum videte
Regem Angelorum:

Venite adoremus,
Venite adoremus,
Venite adoremus
Dominum.

2. Deum de Deo,
  Lumen de Lumine,
Gestant puellae viscera;
Deum verum,
Genitum non factum:

  Venite, &c.

3. Cantet nunc io
  Chorus Angelorum;
Cantet nunc aula celestium,
Gloria
In excelsis Deo:

  Venite, &c.

4. Ergo qui natus
  Die hodierna,
Jesu, tibi sit gloria:
Patris aeterni
Verbum caro factum!

  Venite, &c.

The Latin words and tune of this famous hymn came
into use in the services of the Roman church during the
18th century, but authorship of both is still doubtful; the
original Latin words had 'adorate' for 'adoremus.' The
English translation by Frederick Oakeley was first
published in 1852. The Descant by M. H. may be used
as a trumpet obligato.

30. O Leave Your Sheep

O LEAVE your sheep, your lambs that follow after,
   O leave the brook, the pasture and the crook;
No longer weep; turn weeping into laughter,
O shepherds seek your goal!
Your Lord, your Lord, your Lord, who cometh to console!

2. You'll find Him laid within a simple stable,
   A babe new-born, in poverty forlorn,
   In love arrayed, a love so deep 'tis able
   To search the night for you:
   'Tis He! 'tis He! 'tis He, 'tis He, the Shepherd true!

3. O kings so great! A light is streaming o'er you
   More radiant far than diadem or star;
   Forgo your state; a baby lies before you,
   Whose wonder shall be told:
   Bring myrrh, bring myrrh, bring myrrh, bring frankincense and gold!

QUITTEZ, pasteurs, et brebis et houlette,
    Votre hameau et le soin du troupeau;
Changez vos pleurs en une joie parfaite;
Allez tous adorer
Un Dieu, un Dieu, un Dieu qui vient vous consoler.

2. Vous le verrez couché dans une étable,
   Comme un enfant nu, pauvre et languissant;
   Reconnaissez son amour ineffable
   Pour nous venir chercher:
   Il est, il est, il est le fidèle berger!

3. Rois d'Orient, l'étoile vous éclaire;
   A ce grand Roi rendez hommage et foi;
   L'astre brilliant vous mène à la lumière
   De ce soleil naissant:
   Offrez, offrez, offrez l'or, la myrrhe et l'encens.

The French words and tune are traditional 18th century.
The English translation by Alice Raleigh is reprinted by
permission of Edwin Ashdown Ltd.

31. O Little Town of Bethlehem

O little town of Bethlehem,
     How still we see thee lie!
Above thy deep and dreamless sleep
The silent stars go by.
Yet in thy dark streets shineth
The everlasting light;
The hopes and fears of all the years
Are met in thee to-night.

2. O morning stars, together
   Proclaim the holy birth,
   And praises sing to God the King,
   And peace to men on earth;
   For Christ is born of Mary;
   And gathered all above,
   While mortals sleep, the angels keep
   Their watch of wondering love.

3. How silently, how silently,
   The wondrous gift is given
   So God imparts to human hearts
   The blessings of his heaven.
   No ear may hear his coming;
   But in this world of sin,
   Where meek souls will receive him, still
   The dear Christ enters in.

*4. Where children pure and happy
   Pray to the blessèd Child,
   Where misery cries out to Thee,
   Son of the mother mild;
   Where charity stands watching
   And faith holds wide the door,
   The dark night wakes, the glory breaks,
   And Christmas comes once more.

5. O holy Child of Bethlehem,
   Descend to us, we pray;
   Cast out our sin, and enter in,
   Be born in us today.
   We hear the Christmas angels
   The great glad tidings tell:
   O come to us, abide with us,
   Our Lord Emmanuel.

Words by Phillips Brooks, 1868, written for the use of
his Sunday School in Philadelphia. Tune 'Forest Green'
arranged by R. Vaughan Williams, 1906, is reprinted
from the *English Hymnal* by permission of the Oxford
University Press; harmony altered in third line to fit
descant by Sir Thomas Armstrong (Exeter Cathedral
1949), reprinted by permission of the Royal School of
Church Music. E♭ in last line is for descant verses only.

32. O Little One Sweet

O Little One sweet, O Little One mild,
  Thy Father's purpose thou hast fulfilled;
Thou cam'st from heaven to mortal ken,
Equal to be with us poor men,
O Little One sweet, O Little One mild.

2. O Little One sweet, O Little One mild,
   With joy thou hast the whole world filled;
   Thou camest here from heaven's domain,
   To bring men comfort in their pain,
   O Little One sweet, O Little One mild.

*3. O Little One sweet, O Little One mild,
   In thee Love's beauties are all distilled;
   Then light in us thy love's bright flame,
   That we may give thee back the same,
   O Little One sweet, O Little One mild.

4. O Little One sweet, O Little One mild,
   Help us to do as thou hast willed.
   Lo, all we have belongs to thee!
   Ah, keep us in our fealty!
   O Little One sweet, O Little One mild.

O Jesulein süss, O Jesulein mild,
  Des Vaters Willen hast du erfüllt.
Bist kommen aus dem Himmelreich
Uns armen Menschen worden gleich,
O Jesulein süss, O Jesulein mild.

2. O Jesulein süss, O Jesulein mild,
   Des Vaters Zorn hast du gestillt.
   Du zählst für uns all unsere Schild
   Und schaffst uns deines Vaters Huld,
   O Jesulein süss, O Jesulein mild.

3. O Jesulein süss, O Jesulein mild,
   Du bist der Lieb' ein Ebenbild.
   Zünd an in uns der Liebe Flamm
   Dass wir dich lieben allzusamm!
   O Jesulein süss, O Jesulein mild.

German words and tune by S. Scheidt, 1650; English
version reprinted from the *Oxford Book of Carols* by
permission of the Oxford University Press. The tune is
harmonised by J. S. Bach, 1736.

33. On Christmas Night

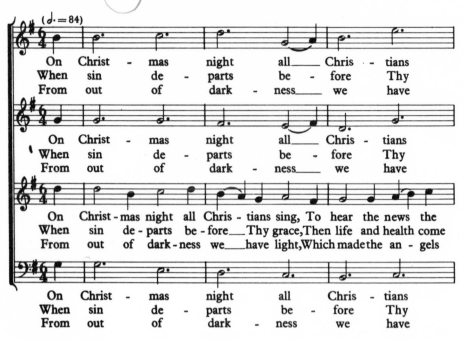

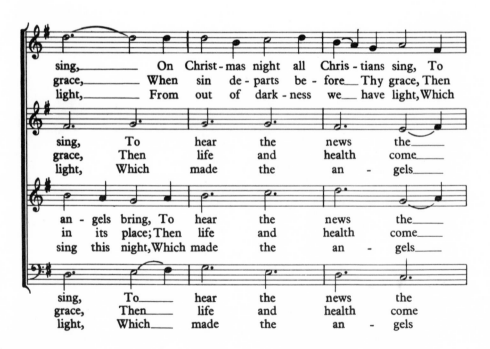

hear the news__ the an-gels bring; News of great joy, news of__ great
life and health come in its place; An - gels and men with joy__ may
made the an - gels sing this night: Glo - ry to God and peace__ to

an - gels bring;____ News of____ great
in its place;____ An - gels____ may
sing this night:____ Glo - ry to

an - gels bring;____ News of____ great
in its place;____ An - gels____ may
sing this night:____ Glo - ry to

an - gels bring;____ News of____ great
in its place;____ An - gels____ may
sing this night:____ Glo - ry to

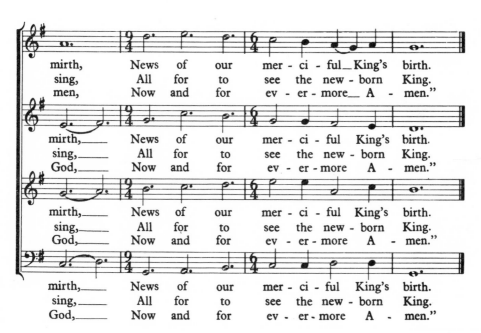

mirth, News of our mer - ci - ful_King's birth.
sing, All for to see the new - born King.
men, Now and for ev - er-more__ A - men."

mirth,____ News of our mer - ci - ful King's birth.
sing,____ All for to see the new - born King.
God,____ Now and for ev - er-more A - men."

mirth,____ News of our mer - ci - ful King's birth.
sing,____ All for to see the new - born King.
God,____ Now and for ev - er-more A - men."

mirth,____ News of our mer - ci - ful King's birth.
sing,____ All for to see the new - born King.
God,____ Now and for ev - er - more A - men."

Words and tune collected by R. Vaughan Williams in
Sussex; this arrangement for unaccompanied singing is
from *Eight Traditional Carols* (Vaughan Williams) and is
printed by permission of Stainer and Bell Ltd.

34. Once in Royal David's City

ONCE in royal David's city
Stood a lowly cattle shed,
Where a mother laid her Baby
In a manger for His bed;
Mary was that Mother mild,
Jesus Christ her little Child.

2. He came down to earth from Heaven
Who is God and Lord of all,
And His shelter was a stable,
And His cradle was a stall;
With the poor, and mean, and lowly,
Lived on earth our Saviour Holy.

*3. And, through all His wondrous Childhood,
He would honour and obey,
Love, and watch the lowly Maiden,
In whose gentle arms he lay:
Christian children all must be
Mild, obedient, good as He.

*4. For He is our childhood's pattern,
Day by day like us He grew,
He was little, weak, and helpless,
Tears and smiles like us He knew:
And He feeleth for our sadness,
And He shareth in our gladness.

5. And our eyes at last shall see Him,
Through His own redeeming love,
For that Child so dear and gentle
Is our Lord in Heav'n above;
And He leads His children on
To the place where He is gone.

6. Not in that poor lowly stable,
With the oxen standing by,
We shall see Him; but in Heaven,
Set at God's right hand on high;
When like stars His children crown'd
All in white shall wait around.

Words by Mrs C. F. Alexander, *Hymns for Little Children*, 1848. Tune 'Irby' by H. J. Gauntlett, 1858.

35. O Thou Joyful Time

O thou joy-ful time,— O thou ho - ly time,—Christ - mas
bles - sings and grace you bring.
Chris - tian— men,— re - joice and sing.

O thou joyful time, O thou holy time,
Christmas blessings and grace you bring.

1. Nought can enslave us,
   Christ comes to save us:
   Christian men, rejoice and sing.

2. Christ now appeareth
   Our sins He beareth:

3. Heavenly voices,
   Each one rejoices:

O du fröhliche, O du selige
Gnadenbringende Weinachtszeit.

1. Welt ging verloren,
   Christ ist geboren:
   Freue dich, O Christenheit!

2. Christ ist erschienen,
   Uns zu versühnen:

3. Himmlische Chöre
   Jauchzen die Ehre:

The first verse of the German words was written in 1803 by Johannes Daniel Falk, a professional diplomat; the second and third were added later in the century by unknown authors. The tune is that of a Sicilian folk song, *O Sanctissima*. English translation by Iris Holland Rogers, 1961.

36. Past Three a Clock

Past three a clock, And a cold fro-sty morn - ing; Past three a clock: Good mor-row, mas-ters all. End

Past three a clock,

Past three a clock,
And a cold frosty morning;
Past three a clock:
Good morrow, masters all.

BORN is a baby,
Gentle as maybe,
Son of th'eternal
Father supernal:

2. Seraph quire singeth,
Angel bell ringeth:
Hark how they rime it,
Time it, and chime it.

3. Mid earth rejoices
Hearing such voices
Ne'ertofore só well
Carolling *Nowell*:

4. Light out of star-land
Leadeth from far land
Princes, to meet him,
Worship and greet him.

5. Myrrh from full coffer,
Incense they offer:
Nor is the golden
Nugget withholden:

6. Thus they: I pray you,
Up, sirs, nor stay you
Till ye confess him
Likewise, and bless him:

Words (except for the refrain, which belongs properly to the tune) are by G. R. Woodward, with two verses omitted; the traditional tune, *London Waits*, is set by Charles Wood. Both words and setting are reprinted from the *Cambridge Carol Book* by permission of the S.P.C.K.

37. Quem Pastores

QUEM pastores laudavere,
   Quibus angeli dixere,
'Absit vòbis jam timere,
Natus est rex glòriae.'

2. Ad quem magi ambulabant,
   Aurum, thus, myrrham portabant,
Immolabant haec sincere
Nato regi gloriae.

3. Christo regi, Deo nato,
   Per Mariam nobis dato,
Merito resonet vere
Laus, honor et gloria.

HIM the shepherds praised in glory
   When the angels told their story:
'Do not fear, but worship duly,
Christ is born, the King of kings.'

2. To Him wise men brought their treasure,
   Myrrh, gold, incense for His pleasure:
Precious gifts they offered truly
To their Lord, the King of kings.

3. God on earth and King of heaven,
   Through the blessed Virgin given,
May we sing His praises fully,
Laud and honour to the King.

Latin words and tune first appear together in Germany,
1555. English translation by Iris Holland Rogers, 1962.

38. Silent Night

(♩. = 60)

SILENT night, holy night,
All is calm, all is bright;
Round yon virgin mother and Child,
Holy Infant so tender and mild,
Sleep in heavenly peace,
Sleep in heavenly peace.

2. Silent night, holy night,
Shepherds quake at the sight;
Glories stream from heaven afar,
Heavenly hosts sing Alleluia:
Christ the Saviour is born!
Christ the Saviour is born!

3. Silent night, holy night,
Son of God, love's pure light;
Radiance beams from Thy holy face,
With the dawn of redeeming grace,
Jesus, Lord, at Thy birth.
Jesus, Lord, at Thy birth.

STILLE Nacht, heilige Nacht!
Alles schläft, einsam wacht
Nur das traute, hochheilige Paar.
Holder Knabe im lockigen Haar,
Schlaf in himmlischer Ruh,
Schlaf in himmlischer Ruh!

2. Stille Nacht, heilige Nacht!
Hirten erst kund gemacht,
Durch der Engel Halleluja
Tönt es laut von fern und nah:
Christ, der Retter, ist da,
Christ, der Retter, ist da!

3. Stille Nacht, heilige Nacht!
Gottes Sohn, O wie lacht
Lieb' aus deinem göttlichen Mund,
Da uns schlägt die rettende Stund,
Christ, in deiner Geburt,
Christ, in deiner Geburt!

Words by Joseph Mohr, tune by Franz Gruber, written
together for Christmas 1818. This English version is
anonymous, first appearing in print in the *Sunday
School Hymnal*, 1871.

39. Sans Day Carol

And Ma - ry bore sweet Je-sus Christ our Sa - viour for to be, And the first tree in the green-wood, it was the hol - ly, Hol - ly! Hol - ly! And the first tree in the green-wood, it was the hol - ly.

NOW the holly bears a berry as white as the milk,
And Mary bore Jesus Christ who was wrapped up in silk:

And Mary bore sweet Jesus Christ our Saviour for to be,
And the first tree in the greenwood, it was the holly,
Holly! Holly!
And the first tree in the greenwood, it was the holly.

2. Now the holly bears a berry as green as the grass,
And Mary bore Jesus, who died on the cross:

3. Now the holly bears a berry as black as the coal,
And Mary bore Jesus, who died for us all:

4. Now the holly bears a berry, as blood it is red,
Then trust we our Saviour, who rose from the dead:

Called 'Sans Day' or 'St Day' because it was first taken
down at St Day in the parish of Gwennap, Cornwall.
Words and tune reprinted from the *Oxford Book of
Carols* by permission of the Oxford University Press.

40. The First Nowell

(♩=160)

No - well,___ No - well, No - well, No -

-well,___ Born is the King___ of Is - ra - el.

THE first Nowell the Angel did say
Was to certain poor shepherds in fields as they lay:
In fields where they lay keeping their sheep,
On a cold winter's night that was so deep.

Nowell, Nowell, Nowell, Nowell,
Born is the King of Israel.

2. They lookèd up and saw a star,
    Shining in the east, beyond them far,
    And to the earth it gave great light,
    And so it continued both day and night:

*3. And by the light of that same star,
    Three Wise Men came from country far;
    To seek for a king was their intent,
    And to follow the star wherever it went:

4. This star drew nigh to the north-west,
    O'er Bethlehem it took its rest,
    And there it did both stop and stay,
    Right over the place where Jesus lay.

*5. Then entered in those Wise Men three,
    Full reverently upon their knee,
    And offered there, in his presence,
    Their gold and myrrh and frankincense:

6. Then let us all with one accord
    Sing praises to our heavenly Lord,
    That hath made heaven and earth of nought,
    And with his blood mankind hath bought.

Words and tune traditional, probably not later than the
17th century; the tune may be a descant for another tune
now lost. Harmony by Sir John Stainer.

63

41. The Holly and the Ivy

The hol-ly and the i-vy, When they are both full grown, Of all the trees that are in the wood, The hol ly bears the crown.

The ris-ing of the sun And the run-ning of the deer, The play-ing of the mer-ry or-gan, Sweet sing-ing in the choir.

THE holly and the ivy,
   When they are both full grown,
Of all the trees that are in the wood,
The holly bears the crown:

   *The rising of the sun
   And the running of the deer,
   The playing of the merry organ,
   Sweet singing in the choir.*

2. The holly bears a blossom,
   As white as the lily flower,
   And Mary bore sweet Jesus Christ
   To be our sweet Saviour:

3. The holly bears a berry,
   As red as any blood,
   And Mary bore sweet Jesus Christ
   To do us sinners good:

*4. The holly bears a prickle,
   As sharp as any thorn,
   And Mary bore sweet Jesus Christ
   On Christmas day in the morn:

*5. The holly bears a bark,
   As bitter as any gall,
   And Mary bore sweet Jesus Christ
   For to redeem us all:

6. The holly and the ivy,
   When they are both full grown,
   Of all the trees that are in the wood,
   The holly bears the crown:

Words and tune collected in Gloucestershire by Cecil Sharp, and reprinted by permission of Novello & Co. Ltd.

42. The Infant King

SING lullaby!
  Lullaby baby, now a-sleeping,
Sing lullaby!
Hush, do not wake the Infant King.
Soon will come sorrow with the morning,
Soon will come bitter grief and weeping:
Sing lullaby!

2. Sing lullaby!
  Lullaby baby, now a-sleeping,
Sing lullaby!
Hush, do not wake the Infant King.
Soon will come sorrow with the morning,
Soon will come bitter grief and weeping:
Sing lullaby!

3. Sing lullaby!
  Lullaby baby, now a-dozing,
Sing lullaby!
Hush, do not wake the Infant King.
Soon comes the cross, the nails, the piercing,
Then in the grave at last reposing:
Sing lullaby!

4. Sing lullaby!
  Lullaby! is the babe a-waking?
Sing lullaby!
Hush, do not stir the Infant King,
Dreaming of Easter, gladsome morning,
Conquering Death, its bondage breaking:
Sing lullaby!

Words, by S. Baring-Gould from the Basque, tune, and
setting by Edgar Pettman reprinted from *The University
Carol Book* by permission of H. Freeman & Co.

43. The Moon Shines Bright

(♩ = 72)

THE moon shines bright, and the stars give a light;
  A little before it was day
Our Lord, our God, he called on us,
And bid us awake and pray.

2. Awake, awake, good people all;
Awake, and you shall hear,
Our Lord, our God died on the cross
For us whom he loved so dear.

*3. O fair, O fair Jerusalem,
When shall I come to thee?
When shall my sorrows have an end,
Thy joy that I may see.

*4. The fields were green as green could be,
When from his glorious seat
Our Lord, our God, he watered us
With his heavenly dew so sweet.

5. And for the saving of our souls
Christ died upon the cross;
We ne'er shall do for Jesus Christ
As he hath done for us.

6. The life of man is but a span
And cut down in its flower;
We are here today and tomorrow are gone,
The creatures of an hour.

7. My song is done, I must be gone
And stay no longer here,
God bless you all, both great and small,
And send you a happy New Year.

Words and music traditional English; this favourite
carol has, however, little enough relevance to Christmas.

44. The Seven Joys of Mary

THE first good joy that Mary had,
  It was the joy of one;
To see the blessed Jesus Christ,
When he was first her son.
When he was first her son, Good Lord;
And happy may we be:

  Praise Father, Son, and Holy Ghost
  To all eternity.

2. The next good joy that Mary had,
   It was the joy of two;
   To see her own son Jesus Christ
   Making the lame to go.
   Making the lame to go, Good Lord,
   And happy may we be:

3. The next good joy that Mary had,
   It was the joy of three;
   To see her own son Jesus Christ
   Making the blind to see.
   Making the blind to see, Good Lord;
   And happy may we be:

4. The next good joy that Mary had,
   It was the joy of four;
   To see her own son Jesus Christ
   Reading the Bible o'er.
   Reading the Bible o'er, Good Lord;
   And happy may we be:

5. The next good joy that Mary had,
   It was the joy of five;
   To see her own son Jesus Christ
   Bringing the dead alive.
   Bringing the dead alive, Good Lord;
   And happy may we be:

6. The next good joy that Mary had,
   It was the joy of six;
   To see her own son Jesus Christ
   Upon the crucifix.
   Upon the crucifix, Good Lord;
   And happy may we be:

7. The next good joy that Mary had
   It was the joy of seven;
   To see her own son Jesus Christ
   Ascending into Heaven.
   Ascending into Heaven, Good Lord;
   And happy may we be:

Words and tune traditional English.

45. This is the Truth Sent from Above

THIS is the truth sent from above,
The truth of God, the God of love;
Therefore don't turn me from your door,
But hearken all both rich and poor.

2. The first thing which I do relate
Is that God did man create,
The next thing which to you I'll tell:
Woman was made with man to dwell.

3. Then after this 'twas God's own choice,
To place them both in Paradise,
There to remain from evil free,
Except they ate of such a tree.

4. And they did eat, which was a sin,
And thus their ruin did begin;
Ruined themselves, both you and me,
And all of their posterity.

5. Thus we were heirs to endless woes,
Till God the Lord did interpose,
And so a promise soon did run
That He would redeem us by His Son.

Words and tune collected in Herefordshire by R. Vaughan
Williams. Setting reprinted from *Eight Traditional
English Carols* (Vaughan Williams) by permission of
Stainer & Bell Ltd.

46. The Twelve Days of Christmas

Third day of Christ-mas my true love sent to me Three French Hens,

Two Tur-tle Doves and a Par-tridge in a Pear Tree. On the

Fourth day of Christ-mas my true love sent to me

Four Cal-ling Birds, Three French Hens, Two Tur-tle Doves and a

Par-tridge in a Pear Tree. On the Fifth day of Christ-mas my true love sent to me Five Gold Rings, Four Cal-ling Birds, Three French Hens, Two Tur-tle Doves and a Par-tridge in a Pear Tree. On the Sixth day of Christ-mas my true love sent to me

Words and music of this ancient counting song were first recorded in 1909 by Frederic Austin as 'current in my family.' This simplified version of his setting is printed by permission of Novello & Co. Ltd.

47. Wassail, Wassail all Over the Town!

WASSAIL, wassail, all over the town!
Our toast it is white, and our ale it is brown,
Our bowl it is made of the white maple tree:
With the wassailing bowl we'll drink to thee.

2. So here is to Cherry and to his right cheek,
Pray God send our master a good piece of beef,
And a good piece of beef that may we all see;
With the wassailing bowl we'll drink to thee.

*3. And here is to Dobbin and to his right eye,
Pray God send our master a good Christmas pie,
And a good Christmas pie that may we all see;
With our wassailing bowl we'll drink to thee.

*4. So here is to Broad May and to her broad horn,
May God send our master a good crop of corn,
And a good crop of corn that may we all see;
With the wassailing bowl we'll drink to thee.

*5. And here is to Fillpail and to her left ear,
Pray God send our master a happy New Year,
And a happy New Year as e'er he did see;
With our wassailing bowl we'll drink to thee.

6. And here is to Colly and to her long tail,
Pray God send our master he never may fall
A bowl of strong beer; I pray you draw near,
And our jolly wassail it's then you shall hear.

7. Come, butler, come fill us a bowl of the best,
Then we hope that your soul in heaven may rest;
But if you do draw us a bowl of the small,
May the devil take butler, bowl and all.

8. Then here's to the maid in the lily white smock,
Who tripped to the door and slipped back the lock,
Who tripped to the door and pulled back the pin,
For to let these jolly wassailers in.

Words and tune collected in Gloucestershire by R.
Vaughan Williams; the setting by R. Vaughan Williams
is reprinted from the *Oxford Book of Carols* by permission of the Oxford University Press.

48. Unto Us is Born a Son

UNTO us is born a Son,
  King of Quires supernal:
See on earth His life begun,
Of Lords the Lord eternal.

2. Christ, from heav'n descending low,
   Comes on earth a stranger:
   Ox and ass their Owner know
   Becradled in the manger.

3. This did Herod sore affray,
   And grievously bewilder;
   So he gave the word to slay,
   And slew the little childer.

4. Of His love and mercy mild
   This the Christmas story:
   And O that Mary's gentle Child
   Might lead us up to glory.

5. O and A and A and O,
   Cum cantibus in choro,
   Let our merry organ go,
   Benedicamus Domino.

Words ('Puer nobis nascitur') and tune from *Piae Cantiones*, 1582. Words translated by G. R. Woodward, and reprinted from the *Cowley Carol Book* by permission of A. R. Mowbray & Co Ltd.

49. We Come to Your Doorstep

WE come to your doorstep
To sing you a song,
Our tune is but simple.
Our voices aren't strong.
We sing of a Baby
As old as he's new
Now welcome the Baby,
And welcome us too.

2. The Babe had no cradle
To rock him to rest.
The arms of the Mother
Rock all babies best.
The Babe had no garment
Of silk and of gold.
Her own mantle kept him
Within a blue fold.

3. Each year as the time comes
We too come along
To stand on your doorstep
And sing you a song.
We sing of a Baby
This night born anew,
For the sake of the Baby
God bless me and you.

Words by Eleanor Farjeon, *Silver-sand and Snow*, 1951,
reprinted with the author's permission. Music by M. H.,
1961.

50. We Three Kings of Orient Are

O_____ star of won-der, star of night, Star with ro-yal beau-ty bright, West-ward lea-ding, still pro-ceed-ing, Guide us to Thy per-fect light.

Words and tune by J. H. Hopkins, Williamsport,
Pennsylvania, about 1857.

WE three kings of Orient are;
Bearing gifts we traverse afar
Field and fountain, moor and mountain,
Following yonder star.

O Star of wonder, star of night,
Star with royal beauty bright,
Westward leading, still proceeding,
Guide us to Thy perfect light.

(*Melchior*)

2. Born a King on Bethlehem plain,
   Gold I bring, to crown Him again,
   King for ever, ceasing never,
   Over us all to reign:

(*Caspar*)

3. Frankincense to offer have I,
   Incense owns a Deity nigh.
   Prayer and praising, all men raising,
   Worship Him, God most High:

(*Balthazar*)

4. Myrrh is mine, its bitter perfume
   Breathes a life of gathering gloom;
   Sorrowing, sighing, bleeding, dying,
   Sealed in the stone-cold tomb:

5. Glorious now behold Him arise,
   King and God and sacrifice,
   Alleluia, Alleluia,
   Earth to the heavens replies:

51. What is this Fragrance?

WHAT is this fragrance, shepherds, tell us,
 Charming our senses all away?
Never such sweet delight befell us
Even among the flowers of May.
What is this fragrance, shepherds, tell us,
Charming our senses all away?

2. See in the night a radiance burning
 Flashes across our dazzled eyes:
 Even the sun in glory turning
 Lends not such brightness to the skies.
 See in the night a radiance burning
 Flashes across our dazzled eyes.

3. At Bethlehem you'll find a Saviour
   Cradled within a cattle stall;
   Hasten to kneel and ask his favour,
   For He is born to save you all.
   At Bethlehem you'll find a Saviour
   Cradled within a cattle stall.

4. Almighty God, eternal glory
   To Thee be given in the height.
   Christmas goodwill, in song and story,
   May they be everywhere tonight.
   Almighty God, eternal glory
   To Thee be given in the height.

QUELLE est cette odeur agréable,
   Bergers, qui ravit tous nos sens?
S'exhale-t-il rien de semblable
Au milieu des fleurs du printemps?
Quelle est cette odeur agréable,
Bergers, qui ravit tous nos sens?

2. Mais quelle éclatante lumière
   Dans la nuit vient frapper nos yeux!
   L'astre du jour, dans sa carrière,
   Fût-it jamais si radieux?
   Mais quelle éclatante lumière
   Dans la nuit vient frapper nos yeux!

3. A Bethléem, dans une crêche
   Il vient de vous naître un sauveur;
   Allons, que rien ne vous empèche
   D'adorer votre Rédempteur.
   A Bethléem, dans une crêche
   Il vient de vous naître un sauveur.

4. Dieu tout-puissant, gloire éternelle
   Vous soit rendue jusqu'aux cieux,
   Que la paix soit universelle,
   Que la grâce abonde en tous lieux.
   Dieu tout-puissant, gloire éternelle
   Vous soit rendue jusqu'aux cieux.

Words and tune traditional French 18th century. English translation by Iris Holland Rogers, 1961. It is an agreeable variation to sing ♩ ♩ in all parts in the sixth and twenty-second bars.

52. While Shepherds Watched

With the melody in the Tenor:

WHILE shepherds watched their flocks by night,
  All seated on the ground,
The Angel of the Lord came down,
And glory shone around.

2. 'Fear not,' said he (for mighty dread
   Had seized their troubled mind);
   'Glad tidings of great joy I bring
   To you and all mankind.

3. 'To you in David's town this day
   Is born of David's line
   A Saviour, who is Christ the Lord;
   And this shall be the sign:

4. 'The heavenly Babe you there shall find
   To human view display'd,
   All meanly wrapped in swathing bands,
   And in a manger laid.'

5. Thus spake the seraph: and forthwith
   Appear'd a shining throng
   Of angels praising God who thus
   Addressed their joyful song:

6. 'All glory be to God on high,
   And to the earth be peace;
   Good-will henceforth from heav'n to men
   Begin and never cease.'

Words by Nahum Tate, 1700. Tune 'Winchester Old'
from Este's *Psalter* 1592; the second setting is from
Ravenscroft's *Whole Booke of Psalmes*, 1621. Though this
is the established tune, do not despise the rumbustious
'Northrop' – 'often sung in Cornwall' – which appears
as Appendix 8 to the *English Hymnal*.

53. Welcome Yule!

Words traditional English, 15th century; music by John Gardner, 1962.

S & Co. 6959

Index of Titles & First Lines